The Parents' Guide to Girls' Lacrosse

Jenni Lorsung

Published in the United States by:
5th Quarter Lacrosse
www.5thquarterlacrosse.com
contact: info@5thquarterlacrosse.com

ISBN-13: **978-1460941706**
ISBN-10: **1460941705**

Printed in the United States of America
by CreateSpace

Photos courtesy of Jeanne Mikulski
Author photograph © Flash Digital Portraits

TABLE OF CONTENTS

To Grow the Sport of Lacrosse

To Enhance the Lacrosse Community

**To Educate and Welcome its Newest
Members**

All for the Love of the Game

1
INTRODUCTION

Your daughter has decided to play the sport of lacrosse. Congratulations!

What? Congratulations?

Shouldn't I be offering sympathy that you're about to spend money and time on yet another activity in your busy life?

Okay. Maybe. But that comes later.

First, let me explain why it's really exciting that your daughter wants to play lacrosse.

By choosing to play lacrosse, your child is about to participate in both the oldest sport in North America and the fastest growing youth sport in the United States. That's some exciting company to keep. Lacrosse has one foot in the history of North America, but it's also cutting edge.

Lacrosse is a sport that was originally played by Native Americans in what is now Canada. The earliest documented game was in 1636, but lacrosse was being played in some form long before that.

Native American tribes used lacrosse less as a sport and more as a cultural activity. Lacrosse matches were used as religious ceremonies, conflict resolutions, and physical training. Tribe members gained speed and agility by participating in lacrosse. That training helped them when the need arose to hunt or go to war with other tribes.

In the 1800s, a Canadian dentist named W. George Beers standardized the game by creating field dimensions, equipment guidelines, and rules. This helped lacrosse become a game that was available and accessible to non-Native North Americans.

Toward the end of the 1800s, Louisa Lumsden, the Headmistress of St. Leonard's School in Scotland, watched a Native Canadian men's lacrosse game and decided to adapt the sport for the women at her school. One of her students, Rosabelle Sinclair, later immigrated to the United States and introduced the sport at Bryn Mawr School, where she was a physical education teacher. Ms. Sinclair was the first woman to be inducted into the National Lacrosse Hall of Fame.

By the late 1920s, women's lacrosse began a huge rise in popularity, with many women's colleges adopting the sport.

Today, lacrosse is the fastest growing youth sport, with participation growing by more than 500% since

1999. And guess what? Your daughter is now part of that, too.

Here's what attracts so many youngsters and their parents to lacrosse as it is played today:

- Lacrosse, as a sport, focuses on -- Speed, Agility, Strength, Stick-handling skills, and Strategy.
- Lacrosse, as a youth activity, focuses on ROOTS, which stands for -- Respect Rules, Officials, Others, Teammates, and Self.

Every lacrosse game should have ROOTS as its primary goal because players will play to their best ability, coaches will coach with direction and understanding, and teams will function as a unit. And even though the focus is on ROOTS, teams that work well together may also get to enjoy wins together.

So congratulations again. Your child is about to have a great time!

If you've ever seen a boys' lacrosse game, you may think you have an idea of how girls' lacrosse is played. But believe it or not, the only similarities between the two games are that players use similar types of sticks, the same type of ball (although in a different color), and win games by shooting the ball into the goal. Everything else is different – making the girls' game a noncontact sport that focuses on skills and finesse.

2
EXPENSE AND EQUIPMENT

Somewhere in every parent's list of top five questions about anything is, "How much is this going to cost me?"

Good question.

Here's a breakdown of types of expenses:

1. **Registration or League Fees** – These fees go to help pay for field space or rental, officials, uniforms, team equipment (such as goals and balls) and insurance. These fees vary greatly by state and community. In areas where lacrosse is new and programs have found grant money to offset costs, the fees might be well under $100. In areas where living expenses are high and players have access to athletic training, turf fields, and traveling games, fees could be up to several hundred dollars. Check with your local

athletic or youth lacrosse association to see what the true cost is in your area.

2. **USLacrosse Membership** – USLacrosse is the national governing body of lacrosse in the United States. USL provides insurance coverage for players, as well as a wealth of resources for people involved at any level of lacrosse. Some associations require USL membership. Youth membership: $25.

3. **Equipment** – If you're familiar with boys' lacrosse, you know that the boys wear helmets and upper body padding. Fortunately, girls' lacrosse requires much less equipment. Here's what you need:

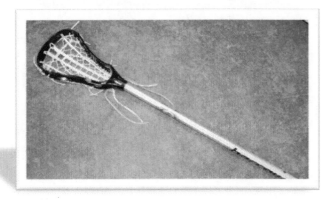

Stick (or Crosse) – The crosse your daughter needs is a stick that's made up of a shaft as well as a head. The shaft can be made of many different materials, including composite, metal, and wood. The crosse's length should be approximately 36" to 43".

The head can be made of several materials also, including wood. The pocket should be strung with 4-5 leather or synthetic "thongs" that run from the end of the head to the neck (by the stick). Between those thongs should be cross-lacing to form the pocket. The heads can also have up to two "throwing" strings in the wide part of the pocket.

Some items to note about women's lacrosse sticks: First, the women's pocket cannot be made from a woven mesh. One easy way to tell if you're looking at a men's stick or a women's stick is that the women's crosse head will have the 4-5 distinct vertical thongs running from top to bottom. Men's sticks will have a uniformly-shaped mesh. Secondly, women's pockets are very shallow – the ball cannot fall below the sidewall of the head. Because of that, women's sticks look very flat from the side.

In keeping with the original women's game, wooden sticks strung with gut thongs are still permitted. They are quite unique-looking, but probably not the best choice for a girl's beginner stick because of cost and availability.

The beginner player needs nothing more than the least expensive stick available. However, you probably don't want to buy even the youngest girl a "fiddle stick" (available about major retailers like Target and Wal-Mart), unless it's just for home use or unless her organization specifically requests it. Fiddle sticks are very small and are not allowed in league play for any age. They also have a mesh pocket, which is prohibited.

If your daughter's stick is too long and unwieldy, you can cut it down so that the shaft is at the minimum length requirement of 35 ½". It's easy to remove the head or the butt end cover, mark the shaft, and use a hacksaw to take off the extra length. Be sure not to cut too much, though, because you'll only be one growth spurt away from having to buy another shaft.

A good rule of thumb is that a player usually needs a new shaft every 2-4 years or so because of physical growth (or more often if you're too quick with the hacksaw). She may need a new head if hers breaks, which is rare but can happen.

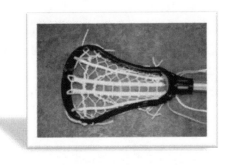

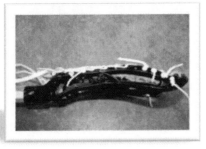

A nice thing about lacrosse sticks is that, within manufacturers, the heads and shafts are interchangeable. If your daughter has a shaft that's too short, but a head that she feels comfortable with, you can get just a new shaft of the same brand. Also, regardless of the brand, if the pocket has become too loose or torn, a head can be restrung with new thongs and lacing instead of replacing the entire thing. Some kids like to customize their stick by picking pocket colors that complement their team colors.

Another piece of advice is that your daughter probably won't need the absolute best, most expensive stick until she can pay for it herself...or until she's looking at a full-ride scholarship to college. National or international athletes in any sport will tell you that equipment that combines state-of-the-art technology with comfort is the best equipment to use. And, believe it or not, it's not always the most expensive. Estimate: $30-$40 for a beginner stick.

As girls get a little older, a great side business is to string heads for their friends or teammates. New stringing kits usually cost under $20, but stores will charge $15-30 for the stringing. An enterprising young woman can make some extra cash by stringing at home.

Goggles – Besides the stick, the next most important piece of equipment your daughter needs is a pair of lacrosse goggles. Lacrosse goggles come in many different types and designs, so make sure that the ones you purchase are legal for use in games. To determine if the goggles are legal, you can check the packaging to see if it carries a note that the goggles have been tested and meet all specifications.

The most common goggle is the cage goggle. Cage goggles have metal wires that protect her eyes and nose from being accidentally hit by balls or other sticks. The have adjustable elastic straps to hold the goggles securely to her head. In addition, they have soft foam padding around the frame so that they rest comfortably on her forehead and cheeks.

Another type of goggle is the visor goggle. In place of a wire cage, visor goggles have ones continuous piece of shatter-resistant polycarbonate plastic. Some girls prefer this type of goggle because they feel like they have a wider vision range.

Visor goggles can be tinted, so if your daughter is sensitive to sunlight (or just likes the idea of looking "cool"), you can purchase a lightly tinted visor. Visor goggles also have an adjustable elastic band and soft foam padding around the frame.

Glasses can be worn under every type of goggle, although it might be worth contacting your optometrist to check into contact lenses or prescription goggles (if available).

Some goggle manufacturers will custom-make goggles in team or community colors.

Mouthguard – You must get a colored one that is clearly visible to officials. This is a relatively new rule in lacrosse, so don't waste money buying a clear or white one because she won't be able to use it. The mouthguard cannot have anything, like a strap, protruding from the front. Mold it properly to her mouth, using the directions included in the package. Consider purchasing one with a plastic case or dedicating a labeled plastic bag for the mouthguard. It will save your daughter (or you) from digging for it in a grassy, dirty, stinky athletic bag before every practice and game.

If your daughter is in the middle of losing teeth like leaves in autumn (like my kids have been for a couple of years now) or getting braces, be sure to fit her more frequently to ensure snug protection. Also, replace the mouthguard if your daughter has decided to turn it into chewing gum. Estimate: $5-$25

Gloves – Gloves are not required, but they ARE awesome! They protect fingers from accidental contact with the opponent's stick, and your daughter will be grateful for it. Lacrosse gloves are similar to golf gloves, but they have light padding along the tops of the knuckles and hand. They also help sweaty hands get a better grip on the stick.

In areas where games are played in cool (or even cold) weather, gloves are tremendously helpful in keeping the girls' hands warm. There are many different glove manufacturers and you can find them in sizes XS-XL. Estimate: $20-40

Currently, there are no set specifications for girls' lacrosse gloves. As long as the gloves are close-fitting and don't make it more difficult for her to hold onto her stick, youth umpires will allow them.

Goalkeeper Equipment – The good news for goalkeepers is that they get to wear quite a bit of protective equipment for when the balls come straight at them! Goalies must wear an approved lacrosse helmet with a facemask, a throat protector (which can be attached to the helmet), chest protection, pelvic/abdominal protection, goalie gloves, thigh padding, and shin guards. Arm pads and shoulder pads are recommended, but not required.

If you've never heard of pelvic protection before, you're not alone! Lacrosse equipment manufacturers make "goalie pants" that have various leg and abdominal pads sewn into the pant. The pelvic protection covers up the lower pelvis area in a way that is similar to boys' athletic supporters. If your daughter is interested in playing goalie, see if your athletic association will provide the equipment.

Cleats – Any lacrosse that is played outside, whether it's on grass or artificial turf, should be played in cleats. There is so much stopping, starting, dodging, spinning, and jumping, that cleats are essential to get good traction on the ground. Any discount shoe store or sporting goods store will have them. A good softball or soccer cleat is just fine. But no metal cleats or spikes! You should find out whether your daughter will be playing primarily on grass fields or turf fields because there is a difference between those two types of cleats. Note – there are "lacrosse cleats" available at specialty lacrosse stores. These are not necessary but some kids prefer them.

Lacrosse Ball – Lacrosse balls come in many different colors, but the "official" ball that's used in games is yellow or orange. Orange is preferable in snowy weather. And, yes, games can be and have been played while it's snowing, although they aren't all that much fun for the spectators! Coaches must agree on the color of the official game ball before starting the game.

Sometimes players will get a different color ball (pink, blue, green, etc.) for at home, either because they like the color or to make sure it doesn't get mixed in with the team's balls if they accidentally take it to practice. A specialty ball that might be worth investing in is called a "soft" or "no-bounce" ball. Although it has the same size and weight as a regular lacrosse ball, it has a soft outer shell. Teams can use these for indoor practices and some families prefer these for home practicing. Lacrosse balls cost $2-3 dollars per ball.

What Else? – With the exception of the goalkeeper, lacrosse players do not wear leg protection. After all, it's hard to run like the wind when you've got ten pounds of padding sagging down around your calves. T-shirts, kilts/shorts, and athletic socks round out the beginning player's equipment.

Some girls' teams prefer to wear a traditional kilt as opposed to shorts. Kilts can be any color or material (as long as everyone on the team has the same uniform).

Some kilts come with a compression short already built in. Other kilts are just the outer skirt and the girls will need to wear athletic panties or compression shorts underneath.

One last thing – don't forget to look online for used equipment. If you daughter is just trying out lacrosse and is a softball player at heart, don't splurge on equipment just yet. Wait until next season when she dusts off her lacrosse stick before she picks up her bat.

If you purchase lacrosse balls for personal use, make sure you label them with your name and try not to take them to practice. Otherwise, they'll disappear quicker than the proverbial sock in the dryer.

3
SKILLS – WHAT SHOULD SHE BE ABLE TO DO?

There are two types of fundamental skills players will learn in lacrosse. They are stick skills and body skills.

Fundamental stick skills are:
1. Cradling
2. Scooping
3. Catching
4. Throwing

Fundamental body skills are:
1. Running
2. Dodging
3. Shuffling

Fundamental Stick Skills

Cradling – Cradling is the act of keeping the ball in the pocket. Sounds easy, right? Not necessarily. Girls' stick pockets are designed to keep the ball in place with a turn of the wrist. This is called cradling. Cradling uses centripetal force to keep the ball in the pocket, even when the player is running. Cradling will be the FIRST skill your daughter needs to learn before she can play lacrosse. Otherwise, a large amount of her practice time will be taken up with chasing the ball that just fell out of her stick.

Your daughter's coach will show her how best to cradle, but a good way for you to help her learn is to put the ball in the stick, hold it upright (parallel to her body), and use back and forth wrist motions to make the ball roll around in the pocket. Think about how a door hinge works. Her wrist and arm should roll backwards and forwards like a door opening and closing. It's not necessarily a big movement, but the stick should go from her shoulder to her nose and back to her shoulder. With two hands on the stick, the hand closest to the head is the one that makes the cradling motion. The bottom hand's role is to guide the stick with a loose, flexible grip.

Very quickly after beginning to cradle, your daughter will figure out how far she can rotate his wrist before the ball comes flying out. And then she'll learn to stop just short of that spot so she can keep the ball in her possession. If you can pry the stick out of her hand, you should try cradling. It will give you a great appreciation for how much skill it takes to cradle and run at the same time!

If your daughter picks up cradling quickly, help her figure out how to cradle with her off (non-dominant) hand.

Scooping – Fact: The ball will take a funny bounce, a pass will be dropped, or a shot will miss the goal. What to do? What to do?

Scoop it up, of course. This sounds simple, right?

The front edge of a lacrosse stick's head is slightly angled to provide a tiny ramp for the ball to roll up and into the pocket. For that ramp to be most effective, however, the stick must be at an appropriate angle to the ground. Imagine using a spatula to turn a pancake. You try to slide it under the edge of the pancake, right? This is the same concept. Only, in lacrosse, instead of a nice non-stick surface, players get grass, dirt, and turf. Oh, and they're probably running or trying to steal the ball out from underneath someone else's stick.

To effectively scoop, a player needs to bend her knees so her stick starts the scoop at a 45-degree angle to the ground or less. She needs to use her arms to provide leverage to the stick so the ball will do its job and run up the ramp. In the scooping motion, the top hand is next to the head of the stick, bottom hand near the butt end, or bottom, of the stick. Both the top hand's and the bottom hand's knuckles should touch the ground at some point during the scooping motion. Once the player has scooped the ball into the pocket, she should bring the stick up towards her head and begin cradling.

Here are three No-Nos that you should watch for:

Raking – I don't have to tell you that kids are clever. When they first learn lacrosse, they quickly figure out that instead of scooping, they can do something called raking. Raking is when a player stops the rolling ball with the back of the stick, pulls it toward himself, and THEN scoops it. It provides a lot of control because the ball is always rolling toward him instead of away from him. But when he applies raking to a real practice or game, you get a kid that can't scoop the ball, run, and get into a position to score…because he's too busy trying to make that little ball roll backward in tall grass or dirt. In addition, once he gets older and other players are allowed to check him with their bodies or their sticks, he becomes a sitting duck as soon as he succeeds in raking – because he's standing still.

> One youth coach recently coined the phrase, "Butts and Knuckles!" Very simply put, it means that your daughter should get both her butt and her knuckles close to the ground before she starts to scoop. Another coach calls the motion "Gorilla Arms" because he wants the players to scrape the ground with their knuckles.

Upright Scoop – Another no-no is the upright scoop. This is the number-one cause of lacrosse-related impalements. Okay, those don't really exist. But the upright scoop is a good way for your daughter to get her own stick jabbed into her own stomach. And it hurts.

One-Handed Scoop – Virtually no beginning player has the wrist strength to scoop one-handed. And even if she did, she has to get her bottom hand on the stick to begin cradling, so it's kind of pointless. Most of the time, the one-handed scoop results in pushing the ball into the waiting stick of the opponent (and losing possession). When your daughter is older and stronger, she can try it.

Catching – Catching is just that...using the stick to catch the ball. At the beginning, your daughter may catch the ball tentatively, like she's catching an egg. But very quickly she'll figure out how much "give" it takes to catch the ball in the pocket and keep it from bouncing right out again. The best hand position to learn catching is to have the top hand to "choke up" on the stick and be as close to the head as possible. Not only does choking up allow the player to have a good feel for the ball landing in her pocket, but it puts her hands into appropriate cradling position. As she becomes more confident, she can bring her top hand down to within a forearm's length of her bottom hand.

Players need to be able to catch the ball to keep it in their team's possession. Possession is critical to having a successful team! So, once your daughter figures out how to effectively catch a ball, she'll be able to put catching and cradling together into one fluid movement on the field and she'll help her team maintain possession of the ball.

A local league requires its youngest age group to complete (or catch) two passes in the air before shooting. The first year the rule was established, some communities' officials gave kids credit for trying – if a pass was attempted, but dropped, they counted it as a pass and let the team try to score anyway. But other communities' officials stuck very strictly to the rule and didn't let kids shoot until they had completed two passes in the air. And when it came time for the end-of-season jamboree, guess who won game after game?

You got it – the teams that made learning to catch a priority.

Throwing – When throwing, the player will learn to position her hands on the stick with the dominant hand close to the pocket, but not as close as when she's catching the ball. She will use the top hand to direct or aim her throw. The bottom hand will stay toward the bottom of the stick, approximately 10-12 inches away from the top hand (or about the length of her forearm), and will pull through the throw to create power. Before a player can throw effectively, she needs to make sure that her feet are positioned correctly. To get the most power and accuracy, the foot opposite the top throwing arm should be out in front and pointed where the ball should go.

There are two types of throwing: Passing and Shooting. Players throw differently when they are passing versus when they are shooting.

Passing – A pass is generally aimed toward another player's stick, about head-high. A pass needs to be caught, so players should learn to throw with appropriate speed and power so that they don't blow each other over with tremendously hard passes that are nearly impossible to catch. On the flip side, players should also make sure the pass gets there and doesn't fizzle out and land on the ground – or worse, get picked off by the other team. Unfortunately, a pass that lands on the ground becomes a ground ball that can be scooped up by the other team.

Shooting – The beginner's shot should start from up and behind the shoulder and be thrown while the player's body is perpendicular to the goal. It's important, though, for the beginner to not wind up, dip her stick backwards way behind her shoulder, and whip it at the goal. You know why? Because the ball will fall out the back of the pocket while she's trying to get that extra power. The beginner should focus on a "3/4" shot – one for which she winds up about three-quarters of the way.

In addition, a shot should be aimed anywhere the goalkeeper isn't. Sometimes that's a high toss in the corners of the goal and sometimes it's a low bounce-shot, either at the ground or at knee-level. Tactical placement of shots can come later when she gets more control over her stick. Then she can learn high-lows, off-handed, and various other effective and/or fancy-looking shots.

Fundamental Body Skills

Running – It's a proven fact that you have to run to play lacrosse. Granted, some positions run more than others (see Chapter Three), but everyone runs sometimes – even if it's just to get off the field for a substitution. If your daughter isn't a "runner", have her run up and down the stairs at home, or ride her bike, or even walk. She'll need to build up her endurance and be sure of her footwork. A good lacrosse runner will be able to run forward, backward, and sideways so she can keep her eye on the ball at all times.

Dodging - Dodging is the art of getting past an opponent that wants to stop you. I think of it as an art because it's a beautiful thing to watch on the field when it's done correctly. There are many types of dodges – head fakes, face dodges, roll dodges, V-steps, etc. But a properly executed dodge means that the player with the ball (let's assume that's your daughter) will outsmart and outmaneuver the girl who is defending her.

Dodging may not be one of the first skills your daughter will use, but she can easily practice this at home – just try asking her to take the dog out or grab the dirty dishes you're handing to her. What she does next…that's a dodge.

> *My daughter likes to dodge me whenever I try to smooch her while wearing lipstick. I like to pretend that she's practicing lacrosse and not just avoiding a goodbye kiss! (Or maybe she just doesn't like the color?)*

Shuffling - Shuffling is the act of running sideways. It's an especially good body skill for playing defense, which nearly every player on the field has to play at one time or another. To shuffle, a player should crouch slightly, like a linebacker in football. His butt should be down and his chest forward and out. While maintaining that body stance, he should shuffle side to side without clicking his heels together or crossing his feet. When shuffling, his eyes should always be on the person he's defending so he can anticipate or react to that player's actions.

In this picture, the player on the left is about to shuffle so that she can perform a roll dodge to her right and lose the defender, who has over-committed to her left-side.

4
FIELD SETUP AND PLAYER POSITIONS

Field Diagram

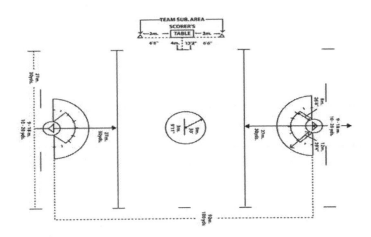

This diagram is for a standard-sized field, but the dimensions can vary slightly for younger youth or as field locations permit. In high school and college field setup is critically important. At the youth level, a rectangular, fairly flat piece of land with the right major markings and more grass than weeds is all that's needed.

Some highlights:

Goal Circle/Crease – The goal circle is the line that surrounds the goal. This is the goalkeeper's home and no other player can touch the goal circle line or enter the goal circle area. If they do, the ball is given to the other team. If a team scores and there is a goal circle violation, the goal doesn't count and the goalkeeper (and her team) gets the ball.

Center Circle – The center of the field is where the draw takes place and is split in half by a short center line. A total of four players from each team line up on the center circle during the draw. One player from each team stands inside the center circle during the draw. See Chapter Four for more information on the draw.

12-Meter Fan – The 12-meter fan is a half-circle line that includes the goal line. The 12-meter fan is primarily used as a marker for umpires to use when determining the severity of a foul and for placing players that have committed a foul.

8-Meter Arc – The 8-meter arc is a line that extends at a 45-degree angle from the edge of the goal circle and out 8 meters. The 8-meter arc has hash marks every four meters, starting from the top of the arc. These hash marks are used to place offensive players who have been fouled by a defender within the 8-meter arc.

Restraining Lines – There are two restraining lines on the field. They are both 30 yards up from the goal lines. Restraining lines determine whether or not a team is offsides. Offsides is when a team has more than 7 offensive or 8 defensive players (including the goalkeeper) in a zone.

Player Positions

There are 12 players per team on the field at a time. They are called: Goalkeeper, Center, Attack Wings, Defense Wings, First/Second/Third Homes, Third Man, Coverpoint, and Point.

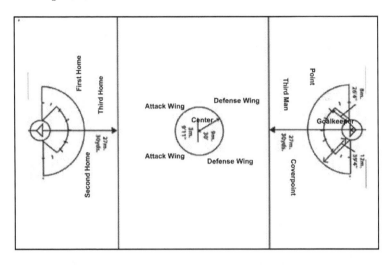

Goalkeeper: Each team has a goalkeeper that plays primarily in the goal circle/crease and defends the goal from shots by the other team. The goalkeeper wears additional padding and carries a bigger stick, just to make it a little more challenging for the shooters. You might want to check with your daughter about the possibility of playing goalkeeper. However, if you find that she's afraid of the ball, goalkeeper might not be the position for her.

Goalkeepers often get discounted camp or league registration fees and/or equipment they can borrow.

> *Goalie can be a great position for a player who is confident, athletic, and willing to come out of the goal circle to make plays.*

Center: Each team has one center on the field. The center takes the draw at the center circle. Centers play both offense and defense and can run the whole field without worrying about any of the restraining lines.

During the draw, the center can stand in one of two different places. She can stand across the center line from her opponent or she can stand on the same side of the center line as her opponent. You'll notice, though, that even when the centers are on the same side of the center line, their crosses are still facing away from each other. This rule is to accommodate girls that are right- or left-handed, as well as girls that have developed draw strategies that require them to be on the same side of the center line as their opponents.

In the picture below, two centers (one from each team) are being put into draw position by the umpire. Both of the centers are fairly tall, but that is not a requirement for that position. There is no right kind of person for this position.

Right and Left Attack Wing: Attack wings are offensive players that stand on the center circle during the draw. They can stand anywhere on the center circle, depending on where they think the draw will go. One of the attack wings' main responsibilities is to gain possession of the ball during the draw, or to prevent the other team from gaining possession. In addition, attack wings should take responsibility for getting the ball moved down the field into the offensive zone. Only one attack wing can cross the restraining line into the defensive zone, however, so the coach will tell the attack wings which girl can cross the line to help on defense.

Right and Left Defense Wing: Defense wings are defensive players that also line up on the center circle during the draw. They should stand next to the other team's attack wings. Like attack wings, one of the defense wings' main responsibilities is to gain possession of the ball during the draw, or to prevent the other team from gaining possession. Defense wings should mark, or defend, the other team's attack wings throughout the game. One defense wing can cross the restraining line into the offensive zone.

To help the girls remember whether or not they can cross the restraining line, a coach can decide which attack wing is the "offensive midfielder (middie)" and which defense wing is the "defensive midfielder (middie)". That way each girl knows whether she can cross into the offensive zone or the defensive zone.

First, Second, and Third Home: The first, second, and third homes are the players that line up in their team's offensive zone, nearest the opposing goalkeeper. On the field, homes work with the center and the attack wings to create opportunities to score. Homes can score goals. They cannot cross the restraining line into their team's defensive zone unless there is a special on-field situation and their coach tells them to go.

Sometimes you will see one of the homes standing behind the goal. Coaches will place her there to spread out the offensive players and help pass the ball around the field. When one of her teammates takes a shot and the ball goes past the goal, she can regain possession for her team by being the closest player to the ball when it crosses the endline.

A trick you can teach your daughter when she's playing offense (but doesn't have the ball) is this: As soon as she sees the ponytail or the back of the head of the girl who's defending her, she should run and try to get open for a pass.

Third Man, Point, Coverpoint: The third man, point, and coverpoint are the defensive players that stand closest to their own goalkeeper. None of these positions should cross into her team's offensive zone unless she has a fast break. In that situation, the coach will yell for a wing or the center to stay back in the defensive zone so that the player with the ball can run all the way down the field and try to score (or pass).

The third man, point, and coverpoint's main responsibilities are to prevent the other team from scoring on their goalkeeper or to cause the other team to lose possession.

5
BASIC RULES

Here's a typical fan experience at a girls' lacrosse game in a community that's new to the sport...

"What happened?"

"I don't know. All the girls just stopped moving and the umpire did this with her hands."

"But what's that mean?"

"I don't know, but I think it's some kind of...foul or turnover."

"But why did they have to stop running? It didn't seem that bad to me."

There are about a thousand variations on this conversation that occur at every girls' lacrosse game. When the sport is new to your area, it's understandable that the rules aren't as commonly known as, say, softball or soccer. Guess what? You're about to be the smart one who can answer all those questions.

The USLacrosse Women's Rules Book is the official rulebook for all women's lacrosse players. The rule book is about 100 pages long, but seven pages toward the end of the book deal specifically with youth players age 15 and below. Although there will always be rules that take time and experience to learn, below are some of the highlights that will make you look brilliant to your fellow parents.

The Draw – The draw occurs inside the center circle and starts every game, each half, and every restart after a goal. The only exceptions are when there has been a foul before the draw or there is a league "mercy" rule that gives possession to the team who is down by several goals.

The draw is done by each team's center. The two girls stand facing each other (unless the umpire directs them otherwise). The umpire places the ball between the two crosses and instructs the centers not to move. When she blows her whistle, the centers pull their crosses up and away to put the ball into the air. Sometimes the ball does not rise above the players' heads and the umpire will give possession to the team that did the draw correctly. At younger youth levels, though, the umpire will often give the centers more than one try to get the draw right.

The goal of the draw is to gain possession of the ball.

Substitution – Substitution occurs "on the fly", meaning that players can go in and out of the game without permission from the scoring table or the officials. However, substitutions must be made through the substitution box, which is directly in front of the scorer's table and in between the two team benches. If an umpire has blown her whistle to stop play, players cannot substitute until play resumes.

Stand – Any time an umpire blows the whistle, all players (except the goalkeeper inside the goal circle) must stop playing and stand. This way the umpire can announce the foul and direct players where to move so that play can resume.

Game Length – Girls' lacrosse games are usually played in two halves and use running time. There is a halftime of 5-10 minutes during which time the goalkeepers switch ends. USLacrosse youth rules say that teams can play with stop time during the last two minutes of each half. If a player is in possession of the ball, her team is permitted to call a timeout, which stops the clock. Also, officials can signal for the clock to be stopped if there is an injury on the field or some other matter that cannot be resolved quickly.

> *Once, at one of my kid's games, some species of large rodent was running around on the field during play. In that situation, the officials stopped the clock. Thank goodness for the goalkeeper's dad, who scooped up the critter in the big goalkeeper stick and released it in the adjacent woods. When we were all finished clapping, the clock was restarted and the kids started playing again.*

Throw – The throw is a term used for when an umpire tosses the ball in between two players during stopped play. The throw is used to restart the game for several reasons, including: a missed shot went out of bounds and two opposing players were equally close to it, the umpire couldn't tell which player caused a ball to go out of bounds, or two players committed off-setting major or minor fouls. When the umpire throws the ball, the two players try to gain possession of it by catching it or deflecting it to a teammate.

Equipment Inspection – At the beginning of every game, the umpires are required to check each stick that will be used in the game. Players form a line and the umpire uses a ball to check the pocket of each stick. The ball must be visible above the sidewall of the stick or the pocket is too deep and, therefore, illegal. A stick that has a deep pocket can't be used in the game until the thongs have been tightened and the ball no longer falls below the sidewall.

FOULS

The rules of girls' lacrosse include 26 major fouls and 22 minor fouls. As you might guess, I'm not going to explain all of them here! But there are a few of each that you'll see fairly often and should know what they are. In addition, there are three procedures you need to be aware of. These are considered penalty administration and are: free position, slow whistle, and cards.

Free Position:

Both major and minor fouls are penalized by giving the player who was fouled a "free position" (including possession of the ball) and by moving the offender 4 meters away. In the case of minor fouls, the offender is just sent back 4 meters from the direction she came. For major fouls, the offender must stand 4 meters directly behind the girl she fouled. You can think of it as a shunning!

There are alternatives to giving a player a free position, depending on where the foul occurred on the field and how severe it was. The alternatives include: giving a player a free position on the 8-meter arc so that she has a good shot at the goal, and giving a card (green, yellow, or red) to an offending player.

Slow Whistle:

Sometimes an umpire will signal that a foul has occurred by raising a yellow flag above her head; however, she doesn't blow her whistle right away. This is called a "slow whistle", even though no whistle is sounded at the time of the foul. The umpire will do this if a defensive player commits a major foul during a scoring play (i.e. an offensive player is within 15 meters of the goal and driving toward the goal to make a shot). The purpose of the slow whistle is to give the offense time to take a shot. If a shot is taken and a goal made, the foul isn't called or penalized. If the offense loses possession of the ball, the umpire blows the whistle and assesses the penalty.

Cards:

Every umpire carries a set of three cards: green, yellow, and red. The green card is issued to a team for delay of game, which is called if a player is wearing jewelry, as an example.

The yellow card is given to a player who commits a major foul that causes, or could cause, harm to another player. The penalty for a yellow card is a 3-minute suspension from the game, which causes the team to play with only 11 players on the field, or "man down." A second yellow card to the same player means that she is suspended for the rest of the game and her team must play man down for 3 minutes.

A red card is given if a player shows flagrant misconduct or doesn't change her behavior after receiving yellow cards. A red card means that the player is immediately ejected from the game and she is suspended from her team's next game. In addition, if a player is issued a red card, her team must play man down for 3 minutes.

Fouls carrying mandatory card penalties are listed below in the Major Fouls section.

In the photo above, the umpire is telling the players where to stand on a free position for the white team.

MAJOR FOULS

Major fouls are those fouls that cause body contact, illegal stick contact, potential for harm, or unfair defense. Four major fouls are penalized by a mandatory red or yellow card. Those are: check to the head, slash, dangerous propelling, and dangerous follow-through.

Check to the Head – A check to the head is when one player's stick makes contact with another player's head. As you know, girls' lacrosse players don't wear helmets. This means that their heads are vulnerable to injury if an opposing player accidentally or intentionally strikes her head. At the youth levels, this foul is a mandatory red card. The offending player is immediately ejected from the game and cannot play her team's next game either.

Slash – A slash happens when a stick makes, or could make, contact with an opponent's body, particularly her arms, legs, and back. A slash can be intentional or can be the result of a player not being in control of her stick. A slash receives a yellow card and a 3-minute suspension.

Dangerous Propelling – Propelling? Yes. This is one of girls' lacrosse's most interesting rules. Dangerous propelling is when an offensive player fouls by shooting, passing, or propelling the ball in a way that could harm another player. For instance, if a first home winds up to take a shot, notices that there is a defender in between her and the goal and shoots anyway...she will be called for dangerous propelling. Dangerous propelling receives a yellow card and a 3-minute suspension.

Dangerous Follow-Through – Dangerous follow-through is a companion to dangerous propelling. Dangerous follow-through is called when a player shoots or passes the ball but allows her stick to strike another player or come close to striking another player. At all times, girls' lacrosse players are supposed to be in control of their sticks and their bodies – both to protect themselves and to protect their teammates and opponents. Like a slash and dangerous propelling, dangerous follow-through receives a yellow card and a 3-minute suspension from the game.

If a player is called more than once for these major fouls, she runs the risk of being ejected from the game (and the next game).

Other major fouls that you'll often see called are:

Dangerous Check – A dangerous check is any stick-to-stick contact that is too forceful than is necessary. At the U15 level, modified stick checking is allowed. This means that players can initiate stick-to-stick contact as long as it's below the shoulders and away from the body. The check should be a quick, downward movement. At 13 and below, no stick checking is allowed. An illegal check at U15 includes anything that is above the shoulders or toward the body or head.

Shooting Space – Shooting space violations are also called "obstructing free space to the goal." Defenders who hang out in front of the goal without guarding someone put themselves in harm's way and prevent a shooter from taking a safe shot. As you might imagine, it's sometimes an umpire's judgment call about whether the defender committed a shooting space foul or the offense committed a dangerous propel.

3-Seconds (In the 8-meter arc) – Once the ball crosses the restraining line, a defender can only be inside the 8-meter arc for 3 seconds unless she is guarding someone within one stick's length. A stick's length is the length of the arm plus the length of the stick.

MINOR FOULS

Many minor fouls can be considered technical infractions. Minor fouls are punishable by giving the fouled team a free position. Seven of the most common minor fouls are: covering, empty stick check, illegal draw, illegal stick, wearing jewelry, delay of game, and 3-seconds.

Covering – Covering occurs when one player guards a ground ball with her stick or her foot. You will often see covering called when two or more girls are trying to get a ground ball. A player's instinct is to cover up the ball to give herself time to scoop it up – but she shouldn't do that or she'll lose possession to the other team.

Empty Stick Check – An empty stick check is when a player holds or checks the stick of a player who does not have possession of the ball, but who could have if she hadn't been fouled.

In the picture above, the U15 player on the right is performing an empty stick check (unless the player on the left had possession of the ball before she was checked).

Illegal Draw – An illegal draw includes any movement by the centers after they've been "set" to do the draw. It also occurs when any part of the draw doesn't go right–a player is standing on the center line, the ball doesn't go high enough, or a player does something with her stick to gain an unfair advantage.

Illegal Crosse – If the umpire finds a stick to be illegal before a game, the player has a chance to fix it. If, instead, she plays with it anyway and is caught, she'll be called for an illegal crosse.

Wearing Jewelry – Girls cannot wear ANY jewelry while playing lacrosse. The only (and I really mean only) exception is medical alert jewelry that is covered by a cloth wristband. No necklaces, earrings, rings, bracelets, anklets... you get the idea. Nothing. Girls may wear barrettes and ponytail holders as long as they do not endanger any player.

A few years ago I had a player who was gauging her ears. For those of you who don't know what that is...you're about to. Gauging means that you try to get your piercing hole increasingly bigger. When the girl decided to play lacrosse she learned that she had to remove her various earrings before every game (which sometimes took a fair amount of time!). All season her mom hoped that the holes would close while she was playing. Unfortunately, we couldn't schedule daily eight- hour games to get that done...

In this picture, there are several fouls occurring. First, one player is stepping on the goalie's stick (covering). Secondly, it appears that at least one player is in the goal circle (goal circle violation). And finally, the goalie cannot rake the ball back into the goal circle unless there are no players near her (covering).

Delay of Game – An umpire will call delay of game if a player has to leave the field to remove jewelry, if she doesn't have her mouthguard placed properly in her mouth, if she isn't wearing her goggles correctly, or if she moves after the whistle is blown.

3-Seconds (Defense Positioning) – This 3-seconds foul (different from the one that's a major foul) is unique to youth girls' lacrosse. At the U-13 level and below, no stick-checking is allowed. So, girls cannot try to knock the ball out of another player's crosse by hitting it. In order to reward defensive players that are in good position to check (if they could), the umpire can call a foul on an offensive player who doesn't move the ball within three seconds of having a defender marking her in good checking position.

Offsides – Offsides, when either team has too many players below a restraining line, is considered a team foul. If an offensive player crosses the restraining line, the umpire will blow her whistle and award a free position to the defense four meters from the restraining line. The offender must stand on the restraining line. If the defense is offsides, the umpire may signal a slow whistle to allow the offense to complete its play.

The players in this photo are all legally waiting at the restraining line.

The player on the far left of the picture on the right is offsides. Depending on whether she's offense or defense, she may be asked to move back or the whistle may be blown and offsides called.

6
DRILLS TO DO AT HOME

I know you were just wondering what to do with all your free time once you're finished reading this book...Wait! Wait! I know that's not really true. But, if you're interested in giving your daughter some ways to improve her skills at home so she can shine at practice, here you go.

Wall Ball – This is the NUMBER ONE way a kid can practice on her own. Nearly everyone involved in the sport, from youth coaches to college lacrosse players will give this as their first piece of advice: Play wall ball.

Wall ball is simple. Your daughter will take a ball and her stick, find a nice flat exterior wall (preferably with no windows!), and play catch with herself. Sounds boring, I know. But it's more challenging than you might think. First, your beginning player will think she should stand about twenty feet away from the wall, bounce the ball to the wall, and catch the ball on its bouncing way back. Yes, that's fun, but not entirely useful. A little tougher variation that will help her throwing skills is to stand about fifteen feet away from the wall, throw the ball to the wall using good form and follow-through, and catch it on the bounce when it comes back. She should practice this as often as necessary until she can place his throw exactly where she wants it and catch it after just one bounce.

Another good way to utilize wall ball as a catching drill is to have your daughter stand fairly close to the wall – even just five feet away. She should flick to ball to the wall and the wall will flick it right back. No bouncing allowed. Just back and forth, back and forth, until she can catch it twenty, thirty, forty times or more without dropping it. Then, she can switch hands and do the same thing with her off hand.

If switching to her off hand is too much to try right away, have her back up from the wall one step and repeat the process with her strong hand. In between throws at the wall, she can practice cradling – maybe giving the ball one quick cradle before tossing it back. If you ever get a chance to watch an advanced player (male or female) play wall ball, watch how quickly he or she can do it. It's almost like watching a boxer work a speed bag in the gym.

Cradling – This next drill is very simple, but doesn't fly in every household, so there are variations listed below. To cradle at home, have your daughter put one or two balls in the stick pocket and cradle while she's watching television. She can cradle with her strong hand first and switch to her off hand during commercials. Variations: For those of you who are cringing at the thought of having both a stick AND balls in the house at the same time, have her cradle a tennis ball or apple instead. Don't let her try to talk you into letting her cradle during dinner or homework, though. Or with an egg…

Scooping – This scooping drill is a combo drill/chore finisher, so be careful how you sell it to her. Here's the thought: Why not combine her devotion to practicing her lacrosse skills in the house with your desire that she clean up for once? To practice scooping, have her scoop up toys, dirty clothes, wet towels, (not dog poop), shoes…anything that happens to be on the floor or the ground when it's not supposed to be. With younger children, this can be really fun (because they don't know you're tricking them into picking up). For older kids, well, good luck. You can always negotiate a bribe.

Running – We don't all live somewhere where it's advisable to send your daughter out running by herself. I know I don't, if for no other reason that the roads and sidewalks are covered with snow several months out of the year. If your daughter doesn't have a place to run where you live, have her find a set of stairs in your house or building and run up and down them a few times each day or every other day. It seems like a little thing, but it will help her get those legs ready to run on the field.

** One note – If you own a baseball or softball mitt, use it to play catch with your daughter. YOU don't have to have a stick to be able to hang out with her. But for even more fun, get yourself a stick and give it a go. You might just find that you like it as much as she does! Then you can recruit your friends or join an adult league...

For more interested families, you can buy pitch-backs/rebounders (usually used for baseball), goals, a fake-goalie screen with cut out scoring holes, special attachments for the stick, etc. Those all have value, but aren't vital to becoming a great youth lacrosse player.

My kids have goals because we offer to store them during the off-season (you might try that with your association). We splurged and bought the fake goalie screen because they each pelted the "goalie" sibling one too many times – and weren't always wearing protective gear, despite my best threats and cajoling. They don't have any other gadgets, though, mostly because they have each other to practice with, whether they like it or not.

7
COMMUNITY AND CULTURE

I'd like to tell you a little bit about what it means to be part of the lacrosse community. And that's what it is – a community that has its own culture, its own standards, and its own identity.

Lacrosse is more than a sport, youth or otherwise. Personally, I think lacrosse draws and retains so many followers because it's not a divider; it's a unifier. I originally became involved with lacrosse because my kids were playing and there wasn't an organized structure. Since that time, though, I haven't become disillusioned or jaded; in fact, I've come to believe in the power of lacrosse as a character-builder and a way of life.

One great thing about lacrosse is that it's an activity that can bring together a quarterback, a sax player, a basketball guard, and a skateboarder. There is a position for every body type and every personality. Lacrosse players gravitate to other lacrosse players and form friendships that transcend neighborhoods and school affiliations. If your daughter wears her jersey or lacrosse t-shirt out in public and another lacrosse player sees it, there's a natural tendency for them to nod to each other or strike up a conversation. Every lacrosse player knows what it takes to be successful − a willingness to work hard and to uphold high standards of behavior − and she respects that same level of commitment in another player.

For parents of lacrosse players, there are opportunities to make new acquaintances and create new friendships. There are also plenty of opportunities to step outside of one's usual routine and become more involved in grass-roots efforts to expand and support lacrosse. As a parent of lacrosse players, I value that lacrosse provides an emphasis on sportsmanship. I know that my children will be asked to be respectful, even while they are being competitive. I know they've learned to recognize that inappropriate behavior they've seen in other sports isn't allowed in lacrosse.

I'm glad there's a lacrosse village supporting my values as a parent.

8

YOU HAD ME AT THE WORD CONGRATULATIONS (BUT WHAT CAN I DO TO HELP OUT...BESIDES PAYING FOR STUFF AND SHOWING UP AT GAMES?)

I thought you'd never ask.

There are so many ways you can help out that I couldn't possibly list them all. But here are 10:

1. Support your daughter by getting her to games and practices on time and with the proper equipment. Learn the rules with her (because there are a LOT) and always promote good sportsmanship. (Remember ROOTS from the very beginning of this book?)

2. Offer to help the coach by carrying equipment to and from the fields or storing it at your house if necessary.
3. Become a timekeeper and/or scorekeeper (it's a well-kept secret that this is one of the best ways to learn the game...because you're sitting where you can hear the coaches and the officials).
4. Take on administrative duties like ordering uniforms or handling registration.
5. Become a head coach. Coach training is available from USLacrosse.
6. Become an assistant coach.
7. Manage the team by sending out emails and making phone calls.
8. Schedule games and practices.
9. Volunteer to be a member of your local lacrosse league's board of directors.
10. Volunteer at the state level or with US Lacrosse, the national governing body of lacrosse.

Within all of those opportunities, there are other possibilities. Carpool, take team pictures, organize a fundraiser, research tournaments, learn how to referee, purchase extra balls for the team, write press releases for local papers...you name it and it can be accomplished and greatly appreciated.

And if you really, really don't have time to help out (and I know that can be the case), the best thing you can do is exhibit and model good sportsmanship every time you can.

We had a family a few years ago in which the daughter tried lacrosse for the first time while she played concurrently on a softball team. She split her time between the two sports. Her dad had been her softball coach for a few years and was a recreational player. Needless to say, they were a softball-with-a-capital-S family. Then his daughter began to love lacrosse.

Let me tell you a couple of final things. First, I've done almost everything on the list above, so I know those things can be squeezed into a busy family schedule. Secondly, you really don't have to be a former player or be willing to create a brand-new program to volunteer. I'm helping out a sport that I never played. So believe me when I tell you that anyone who is willing to devote even a little bit of time to helping out will be treasured – you don't have to know diddly - squat. Just start small and see how you like it.

Secondly, I challenge you to compare volunteering for lacrosse to volunteering for any other sport. I suspect you will find that lacrosse is different because of its emphasis on respect and sportsmanship, and that you will get as much or more out of it than you put in. In many areas, lacrosse is still a grass-roots sport and you, as a volunteer at the ground level, can have a great deal of influence on the "culture" of the sport in your community. Believe it or not, youth sports do not have to be the bastions of politics and in-fighting that they are often portrayed to be. It's within your power to help make lacrosse different than all the other youth sports.

And, best of all, your kid might even skip a dodge once in awhile and tell you thanks. My daughter almost did yesterday.

ABOUT THE AUTHOR

Jenni Lorsung is up to her eyeballs in lacrosse. She is President of Youth Lacrosse of She is a member of the USLacrosse Board Development and Men's Game Youth and Interscholastic Committees and a two-time USLacrosse convention presenter. She is President of Youth Lacrosse of Minnesota and a board member of Homegrown Lacrosse, a Minnesota-based non-for-profit. She has coached 4th-8th grade girls and is the former

Valley Athletic Association Girls' Lacrosse Coordinator. In addition, she is the founder of the VAA Lax Lites program offered for K-3rd graders.

Jenni is a graduate of DePauw University with a BA in Writing. She spent a few fun years as a middle school English teacher in Indiana and Ohio before moving to Minnesota. In addition to publishing credits for poetry, she is the author of "First Timer Frenzy," an article in the March, 2008 issue of *Lacrosse Magazine*. She is also the author of *The Parents' Guide to Boys' Lacrosse* which is the boys' version of this book. When she isn't planning, talking, and thinking lacrosse, she's completing a novel (which only has one lacrosse player in it...so far).

Jenni lives in Burnsville, Minnesota with her family and a garage full of equipment.

ABOUT 5TH QUARTER LACROSSE

5th Quarter Lacrosse is a company dedicated to growing the sport of lacrosse through education and support for parents of young players.

For information on how 5th Quarter Lacrosse can help you or your local organization, please send an email to info@5thquarterlacrosse.com or visit our website at www.5thquarterlacrosse.com for more information.

Made in the USA
Charleston, SC
16 February 2012